MW01595117

Criminal Psychology:

Understanding the Dark and Twisted Mind of a Serial Killer

Damien Woods

© Copyright 2017 by Damian Woods - All rights reserved.

The following eBook is reproduced below with the goal of providing information that is as accurate and reliable as possible. Regardless, purchasing this eBook can be seen as consent to the fact that both the publisher and the author of this book are in no way experts on the topics discussed within and that any recommendations or suggestions that are made herein are for entertainment purposes only. Professionals should be consulted as needed prior to undertaking any of the action endorsed herein.

This declaration is deemed fair and valid by both the American Bar Association and the Committee of Publishers Association and is legally binding throughout the United States.

Furthermore, the transmission, duplication or reproduction of any of the following work including specific information will be considered an illegal act irrespective of if it is done electronically or in print. This extends to creating a secondary or tertiary copy of the work or a recorded copy and is only allowed with express written consent from the Publisher. All additional right reserved.

The information in the following pages is broadly considered to be a truthful and accurate account of facts and as such any inattention, use or misuse of the information in question by the reader will render any resulting actions solely under their purview. There are no scenarios in which the publisher or the original author of this work can be in any fashion deemed liable for any hardship or damages that may befall them after undertaking information described herein.

Additionally, the information in the following pages is intended only for informational purposes and should thus be thought of as universal. As befitting its nature, it is presented without assurance regarding its prolonged validity or interim quality. Trademarks that are mentioned are done without written consent and can in no way be considered an endorsement from the trademark holder.

Table of Contents

Introduction

Congratulations on downloading: Criminal Psychology: *Understanding the Dark and Twisted Mind of a Serial Killer*

The following chapters will discuss: the mind of a serial killer, common serial killer behavior, motives of a serial killer and the theories used to explain serial killer mindset and behavior. It should help the reader understand a serial killer's world, the thought process of the serial killer, and the background of a serial killer. Real life serial killers will be used as examples throughout this book, including men, women and children.

There are plenty of books on this subject on the market, thanks again for choosing this one! It should provide insight into the world of a serial killer, why they do the things they do, how they feel while they are committing the act and how they feel afterward. We will look at the reasons why they continue to kill, what motivates these monsters to seek out other victims and end their lives. Though it is a disturbing subject, I hope this book brings some understanding to the world of the serial killer.

The definition of a serial killer is someone who has killed three or more people. Different law enforcement agencies have different criteria as to how many individuals a person must kill to make them a serial killer. The FBI (Federal Bureau of Investigation) states that a serial killer is defined when they kill two or more persons in separate acts, but not always, by one offender acting alone. Definitions below can vary based on the references and sources used.

Serial killing differs from a killing spree in that a killing spree is when two or more killings happen back to back. Typically, a serial killer has a cooling off period or a time where they get back to normal before committing another crime. Killing sprees are considered one event though they take place in separate locations because there is no cooling off period. Sprees do not follow a pattern—they are usually individual killings not in groups.

Mass murderers are individuals or groups who kill more than four people in a single location. The murders can be all at once or one individual at a time over a period of days.

Killers who also murder multiple members of their family are also considered mass murderers. Typically, the individual responsible for the mass murder ends up dying themselves. Mass murder differs from genocide in that mass murder typically kills people randomly where genocide targets specific people based on race, gender, religious beliefs and sexual preference.

Serial killers usually choose their victims and plan their crime carefully. As said before they usually have a cooling off period before selecting their next victim. Some will travel long distances to find their perfect victim, while others will stay in the same place.

There are four subcategories of serial killers. The first is the visionary. These people, usually psychotic, kill because the voices in their heads tell them to, while others have visions that compel them to kill certain types of individuals. The next is the mission -oriented killer. They believe the world would be a better place without certain types of individuals in it. Hedonistic Serial killers kill for the thrill of killing. Many times, they become sexually aroused by the act of killing. Last is the power-oriented serial killer. Typically, not psychotic, these killers choose their victims with the intent of having total domination over them. They demand the victims do everything they are told, but will kill them in the end.

The impact a serial killer has on a community is also worth mentioning. When the serial killer murders someone, they feel satisfaction, but when that feeling wears off, they typically have the urge to kill once again. Once the media announces that a killer is on the loose, people in the community tend to act differently. The serial killer puts fear into the lives of individuals to keep them from going out at night, or walking by themselves, or letting their children play in the street. They check to make sure their doors and windows are locked, and that motion sensor lights are working. People become more aware of their environment and notice individuals that they might have ignored before. They might keep their keys in their hand when approaching their car to avoid lingering outside of it while searching for their keys. Having security escort you to your car is another form of protection. People trust their gut feelings more during this time. Killers will often try to throw police off by preparing a house to look like a burglary gone bad when in fact, they planned on murdering someone. It makes finding the criminal more difficult in these cases. If your house looks like someone has broken into it, do not go inside. Go to a neighbor, or drive away in your car and call the police. Being more aware and taking precautions may just save your life.

Chapter 2: Behaviors; psychotics or the guy next door

There are many myths surrounding serial killers that have stemmed from Hollywood movies and the media. The myths include things like serial killers are all white males. They are psychos who act strange enough that when they are caught, no one is surprised. The fact is that most serial killers are not deranged loners; some are married and have children. They could be the typical neighbor next door who never even raised his voice to his children and always opened the car door for his wife.

Examples of this are:

The BTK Killer who killed 10 people in Wichita, Kansas over thirty years ago. He was married, had two children, was President of his church congregation, boy scout leader and employed as a local government official.

Robert Yates killed 17 prostitutes in the 1990's. He was married and had five children in Spokane Washington. He was a decorated U.S. Army National Guard helicopter pilot.

The Green River Killer, Gary Ridgway killed 48 women over a twenty-year period in Seattle, Washington. He was married, went to church every week and read the bible regularly at his job of 32 years.

In the year 1929, Germany's Vampire of Dusseldorf killed 68 individuals in various ways as well as committed bestiality and raped some of his victims. He was married, soft spoken and clean cut.

Common behaviors of a serial killer include organized or disorganized behaviors. This classification is made when examiners look at a crime scene. Social behavior is also a big part in determining the type of serial killer they are dealing with. Non-Social and Anti-social behavior is common among serial killers.

An organized, non-social serial killer is of normal intelligence. He is married and has children. He has a normal social life and is a stable father figure. He usually toys with the police and will return to a crime scene to watch law enforcement authorities do their job. This type of serial killer may dismember a body. He kills in one place and takes the body to another location, and the crime scene is neat and controlled. He will talk with his victims, and during interrogation responds best to direct interviewing. This type of killer usually has a history of physical abuse by a parent or caregiver.

The disorganized anti-social serial killer is of lower intelligence. They do not date and are not married. They are socially inept. They have poor hygiene and housekeeping skills. They probably dropped out of high school. This type of serial killer avoids the police but will contact his victims' families to toy with them. He thinks of his victims as "it", not as humans. He leaves his victims where he kills them and leaves a chaotic crime scene. This killer responds better to a counseling type of interview. He has a history of being emotionally abused as a child.

80% of serial killers are male, white, in their 20's or 30's and usually kill women. There is no way to tell they are serial killers. They act "normal" in public, but what is going on in their minds is usually dark and very disturbing. As with labeling anything, there are always exceptions to the rules. There have been women serial killers, killers of ethnic backgrounds and even children who kill. Bedwetting, animal cruelty and arson are the three foremost behaviors in children that may indicate they may become serial killers someday.

Examples of children that murder are as follows:

 In 1993 two 10-year-old boys in London England lured a 2-year-old boy away from a shopping center, they beat him with bricks and a metal rod, they shoved batteries in his mouth then put him on the railroad tracks and weighted him down so he couldn't get up and out of the way of an oncoming train. The boys were convicted of murder, but released when they turned 18 with new identities.

In the U.K. in 1968, an 11-year-old girl named Mary Flora Bell strangled a 4-year-old child for the pleasure and excitement of it. Then a few months later she killed a 3-year-old boy. She was the daughter of a prostitute and suffered abuse both from her mother and her mother's clients. She was forced to partake in sexual activity from the age of four-years-old. During preparation for the trial, Mary was diagnosed as psychotic. She was released from prison in 1980 under a new identity.

Jesse Pomeroy of Boston began his crimes at age 11. In 1871 he would lure young boys into remote areas and beat them so brutally that it left scars that lasted into adulthood. At 14, his mother moved to Boston and his criminal activity continued. Soon after, a 10-year-old girl from the neighborhood went missing, and the mutilated body of a 4-year-old boy was found near a marsh. Police immediately went to Jesse and accused him of killing the little boy. Later they found the body of the girl in the basement of his mother's dress shop. He was sentenced to life in prison and died an old man in a hospital for the criminally insane.

Thirteen-year-old Eric Smith was picked on because he had thick glasses, freckles, long red hair and big ears. He killed a 4-year-old boy by strangling him, dropping rocks on his head and sodomizing him with a stick. After his arrest, he gave no reason for doing it. He was later diagnosed with an intermittent explosive disorder and remains in prison today.

Fourteen-year-old Joshua Phillips was convicted of murder after his mother found the body of an 8-year old girl hidden under the mattress of his bed. She had been missing for seven days. His family and everyone in the community had trouble believing that he killed the young girl. He had no motive for killing her, simply telling the jury that he hit her in the eye with a baseball bat and dragged her to his room where he stabbed her and hit her. The jury didn't believe him and sentenced him to life in prison without the possibility of parole.

The youngest person to be legally executed by the United States court system was George Stinney at age 14. He killed 11-year old Betty June Binnicker and 8-year-old Mary Emma Thames. He told the police that he wanted to have sex with Betty and ended up killing them both and putting their bodies in a muddy hole. He was sentenced to death in the electric chair. His family could not afford to appeal, so he died on June 16, 1944.

The last one is worth mentioning in that he continued to poison people after he was caught. In grammar school in 1961, Graham Young started experimenting with poisonous chemicals when he was fourteen. He idolized Hitler, William Palmer and Dr. Hawley Crippen who are famous vicious killers. He began to poison his family and friends and sometimes poisoned himself because he would forget which plates he put the poison on. He was sent to Broadmoor hospital after poising most of his family and killing his step-mother. He was somewhat beyond his years. He studied chemistry and knew how chemicals affect a human body and how much of a chemical it takes to kill someone. He was diagnosed with schizophrenia and personality disorder. Subsequent evaluations also suggest Autism spectrum disorder. While in the hospital, he continued to poison inmates and staff, one of which died. He was released in 1971 after a doctor wrote a letter saying that Young was no longer interested in poison when in reality he continued his studies and became more aware of the effects of poison on the human body than ever before. After his release, he got a job working in a laboratory that made infra-red lenses used by the government. Shortly after he began working there his boss became ill and died from drinking tea laced with poison. The "illness" swept through the department and many of his co-workers had to be hospitalized from drinking the poisoned tea. Nobody ever informed the laboratory of Young's incarceration at the hospital. He poisoned 70 people within the next few months, none of which died. It was when his former boss's successor became ill and died that an investigation began. He asked a company doctor if they ever considered Thallium as a poison, and then told a colleague that he was fascinated by toxic chemicals. That colleague then went to police and an investigation led to Young's arrest. The police found an incriminating journal in his apartment that he said were writings for a novel. This diary stated the dose amounts he gave his victims and if he would allow them to live or die. He was convicted again soon after, but died one month before his 43rd birthday from a heart attack in his jail cell.

Behaviors of a serial killer include control, manipulation, power, bragging, charm and normal behavior. Some criminals have been diagnosed with psychopathic anti-social disorders. Other killers are described as having psychosis. Though both disorders share commonalities, what separates the two is that psychopaths are manipulative and know right from wrong, while psychotics are delusional. Killers can also be paranoid schizophrenic, meaning they think people are coming after them or that others are a danger to them, so they kill them.

Though there are many types of behaviors of a serial killer, not one is the same as the next. Each killer has a different reason for killing their victims.

Chapter 3: Backgrounds; Childhood Abuse and Neglect

Many times, the background of a serial killer prompts them to commit the crimes. They have had an emotionally, physically or sexually abusive childhood. Serial killers could be victims themselves. Being born with fetal alcohol syndrome or born addicted to drugs could lead to severe health problems. These babies may have mental retardation, nervous system problems, and an underdeveloped brain.

Growing up in a home where alcohol and drugs are abused could be worse. Living with an abusive drunken father could lead an individual to become a serial killer. The child feels inadequate, depressed or has attachment issues. They could have ADHD or other behavioral problems. 70% of serial killers came from homes where alcohol or drugs were used heavily, but at the same time, most serial killers were not users themselves.

Psychological abuse is another factor that could lead to serial killing. Being embarrassed and having feelings of shame are common. Children who live with psychological abuse fear punishment because it is often delivered erratically, nonsensically, and maliciously. Punishment like this tends to make a child become introverted and shy. They develop a sense of worthlessness. A mindset of non-existence becomes prominent because if they don't exist, they won't do anything wrong and therefore they won't be punished.

Neglect is another form of psychological abuse. Ignoring a child leads that child to have no feelings, and makes him or her believe the world is void of feelings. They find themselves possessing no empathy for any other person, thus when they kill they have no remorse.

Emotional abuse scars a child's developmental growth. They lose their self-esteem and the desire to develop a normal relationship with anyone. It stunts academic growth to the point that the child drops out of school. Simply using words can make the victim develop loss of self-worth. It can also make them feel humiliated, degraded, inferior and stupid. The abuser often has an old wound from their childhood that leads them to abuse the people in their lives. They may not even know they are being abusive and the person being abused may not even know they are being abused. Emotional abusers use tactics like name-calling, belittlement, control, and condescending words to make the victim feel bad

Head injuries can lead to aggression, which in turn can lead to behavior conducive to killing. When there is a head injury of the pre-frontal cortex, limbic brain, hypothalamus, or temporal lobe, there is more likely to be violent acts of aggression. Studies show that brain injuries also lead to memory loss, emotional outbursts, and aggressive behavior. Injury to the brain can change a person's personality and reasoning skills as well. 70% of serial killers that were examined were diagnosed with extensive head injuries from an earlier time. This confirmed the link between head injury and aggressive behavior such as serial killing. What we know now about brain injuries shows that children who experience an injury should be examined by a doctor and monitored to make sure there is not deterioration of the brain.

Sexual abuse in childhood can also lead a person to be a serial killer. Violent sexual acts have adverse effects on the normal development of a child. Some of the male serial killers have told interviewers that they were made to dress up like a girl when they were young. Some had been punished for masturbating and made to feel dirty. When an adult has sex with a child it ruins that child's life. They become confused about how a normal relationship should be. The child grows up to be either promiscuous or asexual. Promiscuity can begin very young and can lead to sexually transmitted disease or pregnancy in a young female. As they grow into adults, love equals sex. They simply do not know how to have a relationship without having sex. Many young girls turn to other girls to avoid the memory of sex with a male. Often serial killers are aroused by their actions and gain satisfaction from killing to satiate such feelings.

Families that do not settle down to one location, that move around many times during a child's young life leaves that child no time to establish friendships and therefore they become socially inept. They end up as loners, unable to develop meaningful relationships. Most serial killers are not remembered by classmates, they are bullied or ignored, which leads them to criminal activity to fill that void.

Bizarre fantasies are part of a young serial killers' childhood. Every killer that is interviewed admits to having fantasies about hurting themselves or others. They have twisted fantasies about self-mutilation or they will re-live their own abuses again and again. These fantasies occur more and more as time goes on. After committing his first murder, the fantasy will be of the feeling he felt during the murder and once that fades away he will fantasize about committing another murder so that he can feel that way again. It becomes an addiction.

Usually, during teenage years, individuals who are sexually driven will over-masturbate. Having poor social skills, the young person avoids parties and social events that may lead to a normal sexual relationship, and they become addicted to masturbation, often leaving scars on their genital area.

Acting out fantasies of hurting or killing animals is one of the first steps to becoming a serial killer. 99% of all serial killers began their killing career by mutilating and killing animals. It allowed them to perfect their technique before moving onto humans. Jeffrey Dahmer dissected animals as a young boy, and his father ignored this behavior.

Chapter 4: Motives; Why, Why, Why?

To examine the motives of a serial killer we must break them down individually from killer to killer. Motives vary from person to person, the same as a personality varies. So, it will be easier to talk about motives with examples of the most notorious serial killers of all times. Serial killers need to keep killing to continue to feel the rush they get when they kill. They rationalize the deaths of individuals to make themselves believe there is no reason why they should stop. It all just simply makes sense to them.

We begin with the notorious Ted Bundy. He was born Theodore Robert Cowell. He was a serial killer between 1973 and 1978. He confessed to over 30 murders after many years of denial, but law enforcement officers think he committed much more. Bundy was raised by his mother for the first few years, but he was told she was his sister. She met a man at a church function and got married; he adopted Ted and changed his name from Cowell to Bundy. As a stepfather, he tried to have Ted involved in family activities but Ted did not join them, rather, he was a loner who had social problems throughout high school and college. He later admitted that he couldn't figure out why people wanted to hang out with other people. The dynamics of social behavior eluded him. He became fascinated with sexual crimes, going to the library and seeking out books that involved sexual violence. He began to shop lift in high school. In college, he was dating a girl who ended up breaking up with him saying it was because of his lack of maturity. Bundy became deeply depressed by this. He went back to his hometown and looked up information on his birth, and discovered the truth about his mother. After that, he became more focused and became a manager for the campaign office of Nelson Rockefeller. He graduated from college with a degree in psychology and continued to work in the Republican arena. He began law school but failed miserably and finally dropped out in 1974. This was around the same time young women began to disappear. He ran into his old girlfriend, and having the appearance of having his life together, she agreed to date him. He proposed marriage after a year, and she accepted. Two weeks later he refused to return her phone calls, and he began to murder women in Washington State. Some speculate that he really began murdering people when he was 14-years-old, but this was never confirmed. An eight-year-old girl from the neighborhood disappeared and was never found. When asked about her, he denied it as well as many other accusations of missing people in his area. He changed his story while on death row many times, never confessing to all the crimes he was accused of. Before being electrocuted for his crimes he said that sexual crimes, sensationalized by the media, along with his addiction to violent pornography were the motives behind all the crimes he committed.

Son of Sam is the next serial killer on the list. He was born Richard David Falco and upon adoption by the Berkowitz family, his name was changed to David Richard Berkowitz. He was close to his mother and when she passed away when David was in his teens, he became depressed. He would target single women and couples usually sitting in a car, but also shot two young girls walking down the street. He injured one and paralyzed the other. In the end, he killed six and injured seven. He sent the police strange letters taunting them as they searched for him. A witness to one of the shootings remembered a parking ticket on the windshield of the car that Berkowitz used to get away, which led to his capture and arrest. After his capture in 1977, he said that it was a demon possessed dog of a neighbor that told him to kill. It took months of evaluations to determine if David was sane enough to stand trial. Finally, he pleaded guilty to six murders and received a sentence of 25 years for each crime. He recently had a parole hearing on May 17, 2016, in which he stated that he has been helping people inside the prison. He works with mental health patients, helps run the chapel, leads bible study, and is generally a nice guy. He has graduated from Sullivan community college with top honors. He said in a statement that he was sorry for all he had done, and if he could go back and change it, he would. The staff at the prison where he has served have said that he is polite and compliant and that he was a model prisoner. David does understand the extent to which he ruined people's lives and says that he realizes he will never be paroled because of the severity of his crimes. He wishes to continue to help people while in prison. He was recently transferred from Sullivan County to a maximum-security facility in Wallkill, NY.

Then there is Ed Kemper, 6'9" and 300 pounds, he was diagnosed as a violent schizophrenic. He killed his grandmother when he was 13 because he wanted to see what it felt like to kill grandma. Then he killed his grandfather because he was unsure of what his reaction would be to the murder. Later after being released from psychiatric care (which didn't help), he moved in with his mother. He would fight with his mother and afterward go out and pick up hitchhikers and kill them and then perform necrophilia with them after their death. Then he and his mother had a very bad argument, so he killed her too. He had sexual intercourse with her head and used her for a dart board. He then invited his mother's best friend over and killed her too. He then called the police and turned himself in. Kemper requested the death penalty but ironically was given a life sentence. He killed a total of 10 people.

Jeffrey Dahmer was a notorious serial killer who killed 17 males between 1978 and 1991. Jeffrey was a normal child until he had to have surgery for a double hernia when he was 4. After the birth of his younger brother, and frequent moves, he became introverted, rarely engaging in any social activities. As he grew older, his isolation and lack of empathy became more apparent. He states that thoughts of murder and necrophilia began to surface when he was 14-years-old. When his parents decided to divorce a few years later, his thoughts became reality. He began to drink heavily and dropped out of college. During this time, he picked up a hitch hiker, took him home and got him drunk. When the man tried to leave, Dahmer struck him on the head and strangled him. He dismembered the body and buried it in his parent's back yard. His father encouraged him to join the Army thinking it might help him find his way and make him feel part of something, so he enlisted in 1978 and was shipped off to Germany. While overseas, he did not commit any crimes, but upon returning home he got himself into some trouble for exposing himself and masturbating in front of young boys. Over the next few years, he would lure men from gay bars with the promise of money or sex and get them drunk. He laced the alcohol with drugs and then would strangle his victims, have some sort of sex with them, then dismember them, usually keeping their genitals or skulls as souvenirs. In 1989 he was arrested for exposing himself to a 13-year-old boy. He pleaded with the judge telling him that he had seen the error of his way and that he needed help, not incarceration. The judge agreed and allowed him to work during the day and return to prison at night for a one-year sentence. Even during the trial, the killings continued. He killed an aspiring actor by the name of Anthony Spears. He photographed himself sodomizing and dismembering his body. After his stint in prison where he served only 10 months for good behavior, he began to kill at a frenzied pace. He killed 12 more men that year, but his practices began to involve experimentation. He performed lobotomies while his victims were still alive. He began to eat the flesh of some of his victims. One of his victims, a 14-year-old boy, ran away from Dahmer's apartment into the street screaming. A neighbor called the police and Dahmer told them he was his 19-year-old boyfriend. The police escorted the men to the apartment and just briefly looked around the apartment from the door. Had they gone in and looked around they would have found the body of Jeffrey's latest victim, Tony Hughes. He then proceeded to kill his 14-year-old victim in the same ritualistic fashion. Finally, his luck ran out when police picked up a man on the street with handcuffs dangling from his wrist. The man said that he was drugged and restrained. The man took them to Dahmer's apartment and after finding the keys to the handcuffs, police searched the apartment and found a head in the refrigerator, three more in the freezer and an array of preserved body parts, pictures, and skulls. He confessed to all the crimes during interrogation but pleaded not guilty at the trial. Later he changed his plea to guilty by virtue of insanity. He was found to not be insane and sentenced to 15 consecutive life terms and had a 16th added on three months later. After being allowed to work within the prison, a fellow inmate beat Dahmer and another man to death with a metal bar. After his death, a group of local businessmen raised money to purchase the items used in the murders and have them destroyed. The city of Milwaukee would just like to forget the horrors that Jeffrey Dahmer put his victims and their families through.

Next, we will review the life of a female serial killer. Her name was Belle Gunness. She was born in Selbu, Norway on November 22, 1859. She killed 40 people between 1884 and 1908. She came to America to find wealth in 1881. She married her husband in 1884 and not too long afterward their store and home mysteriously burned down. Soon after, her husband died of a heart attack the very same day his two insurance policies overlapped. His family wanted an investigation, but there was no evidence of wrong doing. She married again soon after that and then came more unexplained deaths. The infant daughter of her new husband died, and within a short time, he died too. Her adopted daughter went missing too. Belle began to meet wealthy men through a column for people looking for love. They would show up at her farm with handfuls of money, never to be seen again. As soon as the brother of one of her victims wanted authorities to question Belle, her luck began to run out. Her farmhouse mysteriously burned to the ground. Workers sifting through the smoldering ruins first found four skeletons; then more and more were unearthed until there was a total of 40 men and children exhumed. Authorities assumed that one of the female bodies was hers, but it was later discovered not to be. She planned her escape thoroughly and drew money from her accounts and disappeared. She has never been discovered to this day. Her motives were to collect cash and other valuables.

One last female serial killer we will look at is Aileen Wuornos, a serial killer that was portrayed in the movie "Monster". Aileen had a brother that was one year older than she. As a youth, Aileen was abandoned by her teenage mother and raised by her grandparents. Her father, whom she never met, hanged himself in prison. He was earlier diagnosed with schizophrenia and convicted of sex crimes with children. Her grandfather began to rape her when she was 13 and she had her first child when she was 14 after having been raped by a friend of her grandfather's. It was a baby boy that she put up for adoption. Her grandfather belittled her as he would make her strip out of her clothes before beating her. Wuornos was having sex with her brother as well, and began having sex in school in exchange for cigarettes, drugs, and food. After the baby's birth, she quit school and then her grandmother died of liver failure. Aileen was kicked out of the house by her grandfather, so she lived in the woods near her home and became a prostitute. Her grandfather committed suicide and her brother died of cancer after that. She began her criminal career with assault charges, drunk driving and stealing a car. She met a woman at a gay bar and the two moved in together. Between November 1989 and November 1990, six men either went missing or were found dead with multiple gunshot wounds. After the two women were arrested, Wuornos took responsibility for killing saying that the men tried to rape her and she killed them in self-defense. She was diagnosed as mentally unstable with borderline personality disorder and anti-social personality disorder and was sentenced to death four days later. Before her death sentence was carried out, she admitted to killing six men and said that she hated human life and she would kill again. She told authorities that only one of the men tried raping her, but the others did not.

Chapter 5: Theories:
Disorders and Typology

As criminologists conduct studies to help prevent deviant acts of crime from happening, it is the deviousness that separates criminals from serial killers. Serial killers usually are not deviant; they kill for more deep rooted or disturbing reasons. These include but are not limited to necrophilia, cannibalism, sadism and dismemberment. Social and anti-social disorders also fit into this category. When diagnosing a patient, mental health professionals refer to the (DSM) or the Diagnostical and Statistical Manual of Mental Disorders. It is a book used by psychologists, psychiatrists and other mental health professionals that define and describe the disorders of the mind.

The first theory that describes most serial killers is Anti-Social personality disorder, also known as psychopathy or sociopathy, in which an individual has total disregard for laws and law enforcement. They are not empathetic nor do they have remorse when they hurt someone. They are typically excellent liars, get into fights and have difficulty fitting into society successfully. Rarely can they hold a job or develop relationships. There is a checklist used to determine if someone is psychopathic in which the high score from the test is 40, but anything at or above 30 is a determinant of psychopathic disorder. The average score for this test is 4. Most people with this disorder do not become serial killers, but many of the serial killers do have some form of this disorder.

Another theory looks at the genetic makeup of an individual. Studies have been conducted to try to prove that men with an extra Y chromosome tend to be more violent, but there are many rebuttals against this notion. Most men with an extra Y chromosome go through life not knowing they have it, and that is good seeing that 1 in 1000 men have the extra Y.

The next theory to look at is called the Holmes and Holmes Serial Killer Typology which categorizes serial killers to fit one of these models: visionaries, missionary killers, hedonistic killers and power and control killers. Visionary killers feel the need to murder because an angel, a demon, Satan or God told them to kill. Their victims are random. They strike only when this outside source commands them to. Missionary killers kill one class, race, or religion in an attempt to eliminate them completely. Hedonistic killers are sexually aroused either before, during or after the killing. Some that are aroused after they kill have sex with the corpse in some way. Power and control killers want complete control over their victims, including how and when they die. Some researchers agree that the categories may be combined and that the power and control part of this theory is why all killers kill. They all desire power over their victims, but again nothing is set in stone.

Another theory is the organized and disorganized theory. The organized killer is a meticulous planner. They plan where each activity will take place, the encounter, the murder and where they will dump the body afterward. This makes identifying the murderer very difficult because of the cleanliness of where the body is disposed. Usually, the organized killer watches the news to find out what they know, or will show up at the crime scene to watch the responders work. The disorganized killers are spontaneous in a killing. They plan nothing, even show up without a weapon. They will find something at the location where they meet the victim to use as a weapon, kill the victim and leave everything at the scene. They don't move the victims which makes it easier for law enforcement to track and capture them. They will usually take a souvenir with them. There is a third category of this theory that is called the mixed theory in which a killer may kill while hanging out with the wrong crowd, or is high on drugs. The FBI created this category for those that don't fall into the other two categories.

Another theory is the nature vs. nurture theory. Abuse will sometimes have a child entertain thoughts of murder. In the case of John Wayne Gacy who killed 33 young boys, he was beaten badly as a child. He had to endure physical abuse, emotional abuse, and verbal abuse. His father shot his dog and made him watch. He also called him names and made him feel like he was worthless. In these instances, some people get through it and never harm anyone, while others want revenge and become serial killers. Nature is another thing to look at. The makeup of a killer's brain may be different than that of a person who has no murderous thoughts. They may have had head injuries as a child. Autism Spectrum Disorder combined with childhood trauma could lead a person to kill. There really are so many factors as to why a person becomes a serial killer, that prevention is impossible. There is not one thing that we can look at that we can say, well that is the magic combination, let's get help for that person. It's a crap shoot that no one wins.

Over 3 years of done studies by the FBI, 29 serial killers were interviewed. They discovered that 69% had alcohol abuse in the family history, 53% had relatives with family members having psychiatric problems, 46% had sexual abuses, and 33% had drug problems. Mix that with neurobiological defects and it shows a potential for a child to grow up being a serial killer.

Conclusion

Thanks for making it through to the end of Criminal Psychology: *Understanding the Dark and Twisted Mind of a Serial Killer*, let's hope it was informative and able to provide you with all you need to understand what a serial killer is about.

This book covered quite a bit in the way of considering the mind of a serial killer, the individuals they target and why they kill. Still, it doesn't change the fact that it is terrifying. Even though some of the motives behind their actions be it physical, emotional or sexual abuse, a brain injury, drugs or alcohol, psychosis or otherwise that they suffered as a child, their actions cannot be fully justified. It may ,however, give closure to family members to have a reason as to why their loved one died.

If there were a way to identify a killer before they kill, to pinpoint someone early in life that could be helped, that would be great. Unfortunately, there is no way to know until it is too late.

Finally, if you found this book useful in any way, a review on Amazon is always appreciated!

Citations

1. http://disturbinghorror.com/Serial-Killers/Serial-Killer-psychology.html

2. https://www.psychologytoday.com/blog/the-superhuman-mind/201212/the-making-serial-killer

3. www.Wikepedia.com

4. www.Biography.com

5. www.crime.about.com

6. www.Reuters.com

Made in the USA
Columbia, SC
01 June 2020

98796595R00022